C0-DAD-056

"I'm not a Military Transition Expert, and Neither Are You"

My version of Military Transition advice

Benny R. Kinsey

U.S. Army (Retired) Command Sergeant Major

M.B.A., B.S. – HR Management, PMP, PHR

Military Transition Advice from a Senior Mentor of Service Members who happened to have his life crushed when he tried to become a "Civilian".

The Military will show you a thousand successful ways to stay in but little to none on how to transition out successfully. Don't rely on your military leadership chain to show you how to transition out, they've usually never done that before.

As Military Transition Advocates, we can hold all the conferences and seminars we want to discuss transition and Veteran related topics but they will have little impact unless we move the needle with those employed Advocates currently being paid by companies to find jobs for those Veterans. If feelings are hurt, then self-reflection may be in order.

Preface –

Military Transition is not easy for the transitioning Service Member, their families, or the potential employer. My LinkedIn inbox is flooded daily with my fellow Warriors and their family members asking for transition advice. Some of them are within 30-90 days of their "out" date and are really stressed about how they are going to make it on the "outside". As a former leader of many Soldiers, my heart goes out to them because I know what is about to happen to their lives. Some of them didn't even know they were leaving the military in 60 days.

In writing this advice, it is not to represent my current employer or former employers, does not support or endorse any institution or accreditation. It is simply a collection of the thoughts and ideas I have shared with countless transitioning US Military Service Members and their family members over the last few years as they have come to me for advice and assistance.

Introduction –

First, my history.....when I retired from the U.S. Army, my TAP (Transition Assistance Program) was not helpful for me, even in the slightest regard. As a transitioning Command Sergeant Major I was learning how to build my one-page resume along with the several E-3 and E-4s to my left and right. I didn't want to ask any questions, well, because a CSM is supposed to have the answers, especially in a room filled with Junior Enlisted Soldiers. It was not a great environment, and it was mandatory, so I went with the program, taught by someone who left the military just a year prior, who was showing me how to find a job when the job they found only removed a uniform and not much else from their lives. Looking back, I wish someone would have taught me how to find a job, 1700 miles from where I was transitioning, and in a non-military, non-government job waiting for me, kind of town, in an economic recession.

To me, one of the biggest disservices we can do to our transitioning Warriors is to have them sit through mandatory transition classes, taught by serving Service Members, still in uniform, who have never transitioned, teaching them how to put a resume together for a job they have never tried to get themselves. Sounds dumb doesn't it but it is happening even today. Until our transition assistance programs start bringing in actual advocates who made the transition from the military to a successful position outside of the military then, in my opinion, they are simply regurgitating what has been spread in tribal wisdom and folklore.

So, for six months after leaving my last duty station, I applied, got rejected, applied, rejected, applied, rejected....rejected, wait, I don't ever remember applying for that job! Tweaked this resume, that resume, create a new resume, how about a resume for this or for that? My Terminal Leave ended and now my Retirement Date is here....still no job, no interviews.

As the retirement date has now come my income has been significantly reduced, the bills started piling up, stress becomes almost unbearable, and I am at an all-time low for self-esteem. What the heck is going on here!!! I did EVERYTHING they said to do. I went from GED to MBA, I have three college degrees, a Six Sigma Black Belt certification, heck...I made it all the way to E-9!!! Why aren't these companies banging down my door like I was told they would be??? I'm applying to jobs where I meet every single qualification they have and still...REJECTED! I even applied to a fast food chain hoping to get into the Manager training program and after two months the news came to my email.....rejected. Awesome.

Funny how just about every major company had banners hanging "Military Veterans Welcome" and we have "Veteran's Hiring Preference" ....no one I knew was being hired, so what gives? Is it just a motto for the public to like that company? Did they make their "quota"? Either way....I am absolutely livid at this point. Oh yea A hiring conference is coming to town, buy a suit, more money, drive down and park...more money. Walk up to the table and be told to apply online...are you serious? Why are you even here?

A lot of you have experienced what I am describing, it is not fun, it is not relaxing, I was NOT a pleasure to be around....at all. I have worked on these transition thoughts for a number of years now and if you don't mind, I would like to share the pearls of wisdom I have been given in the absolute exercise of humility that life giftwrapped for me when I left the military. I should have asked more questions, I should have taken my transition much more seriously, I should have, I would have, I could have........we all know the rest of that.

I have a lot more to share (not now though), such as fitting in your new role when everyone thinks you're just a trained killer ready to snap, or that we all have PTSD, or "you don't deserve to be here" because you didn't do any internships while attending college so there was no sacrifice....that one is really funny...especially to an old Infantry Paratrooper. Nope, during my "college days" I was a full-time dad of four kids, worked 12-16 hour days and graduated college in the only place I could study in peace...the bathroom...for eight long years and four different institutions while serving in new military assignments. Wish I could have gone to my beloved University of Texas at Austin and be an actual Longhorn but kind of had some preventing circumstances (like the US Army said go here instead) that allowed me to graduate from another school instead.

I am sure my story pretty much mirrors thousands of other Service Members who made the transition from the U.S. Armed Forces into the mainstream economy. Some try to venture outside of the box and seek positions in the Corporate America thinking the positions they performed while in uniform would directly convert into positions out of uniform. Others don't stray too far "from the flagpole" and seek employment either with the U.S. Government in some capacity or they will try to work in the defense industries. It's what they are comfortable with and although we like to think we are risk-takers, we really aren't. What I've learned about getting into Government Service is that if you don't have the connections then you probably aren't going to get a position either.

The Decision –

So, you want to get out, be a CEO, and make a million bucks in your hometown to keep Household Six (spouse) happy, and will never move again. Pretty much sums up the dream, right?

My story went about the same way. I always told my wife and kids that I wanted to retire at twenty years. I used to say that twenty and a day was a day too long. Well, then my oldest son decided to also become a Soldier and I couldn't go by the old saying anymore so I came up with a new one. I will stay in the military as long as I have a child in the military. My oldest son joined the Army in 2005 and so I put my name in the hat for promotion consideration to Sergeant Major after turning down the last three boards. Well….guess what? It happened.

Not only was I a first time select to be promoted to Sergeant Major, but I was a "Triple Select" being selected for not only Sergeant Major, but Command Sergeant Major, and attendance to the prestigious United States Army Sergeants Major Academy in beautiful Ft. Bliss (El Paso), Texas! Oh, the joy my wife (at the time) and I experienced!!!! If only we knew what was ahead, I honestly would have just retired at 20 years and stayed right where we were.

In the next few years I relocated my family to Ft. Bliss and attended the Sergeants Major Academy for a yearlong resident course. For nine of those months we didn't have a single clue where we were going next so life was on pins and needles until I was finally notified that we were heading to Albany, NY to become the Command Sergeant Major of the U.S. Army Albany Recruiting Battalion. Albany was not my first, second, third…well…you get it, it was not a choice of mine at all. I was a Southern boy, a Texas boy and was really hoping that after doing so well in my career that we could at least be within driving distance of my wife's parents. Well…no.

So, we went…to Albany, NY. In that assignment, I was responsible for 250 Soldiers and their families along with 38 civilian staff members. It turned out to be a wonderful assignment and the people I was blessed to work with were second to none. I was on the road a lot since my Commander and I were responsible for five U.S. States and oh by the way...all of Europe, North Africa, and the Middle East for U.S. Army Recruiting. You can probably guess by now that I really didn't end up with a lot of time to prepare for my retirement decision while working. Seeing how my home was going to be near Houston, TX and I was currently in Albany, NY , I severely underestimated just how difficult it would be to create a network and to find suitable employment that far away and in a Non-military oriented community.

Well, in 2009, my oldest son told me he was going to ETS (End Term of Service) from the Army, was going to live in Austin, TX and go to school to be a chef. Sounded like a solid plan so guess what I did, yup, you got it...turned in my retirement packet! Oh, the joy.....Oh, the freedom that was just around the corner! I had been in a military uniform since I was 17 years old. Who could I be? What could I do? How much money could I make? Oh the endless possibilities!!! I joined the Army with a GED, went to college, received an Associate Degree, wasn't finished yet. Continued with school, work, life and received a Bachelor Degree! Wasn't done yet, I knew I needed more to be competitive, went back to school and received a M.B.A. Finally, Done! Wait a minute, why is everyone getting this Six Sigma Black Belt thing? Why is everyone getting this Project Management Professional thing? Crap....let me go ahead and get that too because no one is going to beat me to the good jobs....wrong again.

In 2009, I submitted my retirement packet and worked until I had about 30 days until it was time to go home to Texas. After my Change of Responsibility Ceremony, it was applications, two graduating high school seniors, movers, and the infamous clearing of government quarters. I tried to focus on the resumes, the applications, but no one back in Texas really took me seriously with a New York address so I changed everything to a Texas address. A few calls happened and when I told them I was in New York and couldn't be there that next week for an interview all of a sudden I received the "Thanks for applying but....." response. Well, no big deal, if they are calling now we will be fine when we get there, right? Wrong.

Pure Drama -

So, at the end of June 2010, we hit the road to Texas and our very bright future filled with all the hopes and possibilities that all of my college degrees and military experience could possibly afford. June wrapped up, July ended, August ended and now I am desperate. I contact a friend a LinkedIn that I served with and ended up going through five interviews to get a position I absolutely hated. I accepted the position knowing full well that I really did not want to do that job but bills were due, wife was becoming very distant, and my self-confidence was in the crapper. What was I to do? No one was knocking down my door, no one was calling me to ask about my salary needs, no one was contacting me what-so-ever. I didn't really know anyone where we moved to, we moved there so my wife could be near her parents. We moved there because we agreed she had given enough on all the moving the Army told us we needed to do. We moved there because it made her happy. Well, that didn't end up working out, the stress took more of a toll than we could ever imagine and it eventually costs my self-confidence, my pride, and yes, even my spouse.

In my new position I tried to make the best of it, I tried to tone down the high-speed, low drag action. In my head I was going as slow as cold fudge travels but everyone at the job kept telling me to slow it down, relax, it's a marathon and not a race. Finally, after just 90 days, I couldn't take it anymore and they couldn't take me anymore and we agreed to part ways. I made two really great friends out of the ordeal but the real lesson that it taught me is that by taking that job, it really screwed up what I was meant to do in my future employment.

Thanks goodness for LinkedIn. I hopped on the LinkedIn bandwagon relatively early, in 2009. I figured it would be a good way to create some professional connections and not be in a Facebook type of atmosphere. After my 1st job ordeal I went another 90 days without a job. Bills were now going to collection agencies; my kids were in college and we were eating a little as possible. With one just starting high school, we didn't have the money to let him take the school trips, the new clothes, etc. Our savings were gone, My Thrift Savings Plan (TSP) was emptied out and I was now selling our stuff to put food on the table. All the while applying, applying, applying, one interview, two interviews, three interviews and then "Sorry, but we selected a more qualified candidate"....SERIOUSLY????? You called ME for the interviews!!!! How much did I just spend on a suit, travel, parking, printing my resumes out? I got this...I have NEVER failed and I will NEVER fail! Then the bank calls about our mortgage. I apply for Unemployment only to be told that my retirement check puts me over the limit and that even though I paid taxes for over 30 years now, that I will never be able to collect money or benefits for not being able to find a job. Government bureaucracy at its finest.

Well, without going into the gory details, I became a Single Dad with all the bills and privileges that came with that. Now I just lost half of my retirement check and guess what? I still make too much to collect on unemployment....awesome. I was on LinkedIn one morning and saw the profile of one of my previous mentors, a Command Sergeant Major who retired about five years earlier and he looked to be doing quite well for himself so, I sent him a message. It went along the lines of "Hey CSM! How are you? Can you please let me know if your company has anything available....maybe a work from home since you are on the East

Coast and I am now a Single Dad?" Yeah, talk about a stretch right? Then I get a message....send your phone number, so I did. One interview later I was offered a Recruiter position for half of what I made in the Army but it did allow me to work from home and more importantly, it allowed me to keep my house and put food on the table. It did not allow me to pay all of my bills or even address the items that had gone into collection.

I still didn't get the message, I was mad at the world, mad at the Army, mad at Civilians, just mad at everything and everyone. I did EVERYTHING I was told to do and why wasn't it working for me? What was the point of it all? To say it was a struggle to get going would be an understatement, thank goodness, my youngest son and my daughter were still living with me to help keep the demons at bay.

Two good years go by, working from home, doing my best for the company and to honor the Retired Command Sergeant Major who vouched for my work ethic (I found out later I was the first person he ever recommended in the five years he worked in that company), and then BOOM....the wonderful Congressional Sequestration hits and I am laid off. Don't get me wrong, I was still applying to companies in the Houston area during my time with this company. I knew I was never going to get to a higher level unless I found a job in Houston or relocated to Virginia. With my youngest son heading into his senior year now, Virginia just wasn't an option at the time (divorce decree said so too) and glad I didn't anyway since I would have been laid off in Virginia just as well as I was in Texas.

I was tired, looking and looking for suitable employment, any employment. I finally decided that was enough and now I was going to take life by the horns and was accepted into law school. I was now going to be the master of my destiny, my own boss and I was going to learn how to legally fight for Veterans' employment rights, unemployment rights, among other things. Applied for Vocational Rehabilitation with the VA and DENIED so I did it on my own dime since my kids were using my GI Bill. True to form since my Military Retirement, my family hit a major obstacle and was sucked into the world of drugs and alcohol so I had a choice to make, either continue with the next 2.5 years of law school or drop out and handle the business of my family. Obviously, I chose my family which meant I was back in the world of no job, no income, and scrapping to pay the bills, AGAIN. Self-esteem in the toilet again, worthlessness again, depression…. again.

As the saying goes, if I had only known then what I know now, right? So, to hopefully help you to avoid what the heck happened to me, please, please take my advice and no, I am not a transition expert but then hey, neither are you ▨

If I had to sum all of my advice into one single word it would be – N-E-T-W-O-R-K-I-N-G. Every position I have held since I retired from the US Army has come to me by "Who do you know" instead of "What you have done". Don't get me wrong, it got me the interview, and I have blown quite a few of those, but I still had to win over a set Hiring Managers who did not know me at all. I always say a referral can get you to the door but you have to kick it in to get the job.

So here is my acronym for "NETWORKING" and I sure hope it helps at least one person to avoid the wonderful experiences that life got to share with me in my transition to becoming "Benny" and leaving "Command Sergeant Major Kinsey" where it belongs in the civilian world, in my shadowbox.

Now…..On to N-E-T-W-O-R-K-I-N-G……….

N – What are your Needs?

Finances –

How much do you NEED to make annually in your first job after the military? If you are retiring, then don't be greedy. Try to simply match or exceed a little of what your lifestyle was on Active Duty in the military. If you are getting out and not retiring, then you really need to ensure you do some prep work before you get out. Your true goal here is to find a new position in a new industry and then rapidly work your way up in pay and new responsibilities. You may have to start way smaller than your last level of military responsibilities.

Location Restriction –

Is there a dire need that you have to be only in one location? The most common one I hear (and I was one of them) is that due to moving around as a military family you are respecting your spouse's decision to be here or there. Unless your spouse has a position waiting on you in that location, it is something you will need to discuss just a little bit more. After all, the spouse won't be happy in that location soon if you have trouble finding a position you are happy with or there are now bills that have become difficult to pay. If there is just no other way and you have to be in that one location then you will need to adjust your expectations of what you are looking for in terms of career, money, opportunities, career growth, etc if it is just not in that area. I had one Veteran who asked me to help find a job at an almost six-figure salary for them in a town of 25,000 people and over two hours away from a metro city because he was not going to move anymore. I sure hope they found that dream job and could stay where they were.

Advanced Educational Opportunities –

Sometimes finding the job of your dreams isn't the only issue either. A lot of today's technical positions require more education to be able to advance into positions of more responsibility and pay.

An example is that if you are a Mechanical Engineer leaving the military and take a position in far West Texas that pays a lot of money you will have a difficult time finding an accredited school that can give you an advanced Engineering degree without having to be primarily online. Try to plan this out well in advance of your Terminal Leave date.

Multiple companies in that location who hire for what you do! If you lose your position for whatever reason, are there other employers in this location who also hire for what you do? If you want to focus your next career in Security Defense then Phoenix, AZ is probably not a great choice for multiple opportunities. For Security Defense companies, a place like Reston, VA would be a good idea to have multiple employers who might also hire for what you do. In this case your home, your kid's school, would all remain stable if you had to change employers which keeps the family and Household Six (your spouse) happy.

E - Talk to Everyone! Exhausting!

Getting ready for your next career is Exhausting! It is hard work to find the job you will fill upon leaving the military. Advice is to talk to Everyone! Network online, at work, at church, at your kid's baseball game, ALL THE TIME. The job I have today (though a series of events) came because I went someone I didn't really want to go with my wife (then dating). While she was with her friends I struck up a conversation with other folks and one of them eventually became my boss! Networking for employment is like playing the lottery, you never know which is the winning ticket but you have to buy it to find out. Remember the age-old saying "when you don't have a job, your job is to find a job". Expect to put in 6-8 hours a day in applications, research, driving, networking, interviewing, etc.

T– TAP, Timeline, All the Time!

Use your branch's Transition Assistance Program to YOUR satisfaction. Make the program work to help your goals and intentions. If the program is being taught by a former military member who simply took off the uniform and stayed in the same place or even worse, someone STILL in the military, then find a few Military Veterans who have made the successful transition and ask questions! Get to know them, their trials and tribulations so hopefully you can avoid some of the mistakes they made. This is especially important if you are leaving a part of the country and moving to an entirely new area and even worse, (like me) moving to an area that doesn't have military installations within three hours in any direction!

Know your Timeline –

Applying to positions when you are 6-12 months out from beginning your Terminal Leave date doesn't do you any good unless they are high-turnover positions that companies need to fill constantly. If you are looking for a somewhat specialized position, then you will need to wait until you are 30-60 days out from being able to start with that company. Companies primarily work on what they have open right now....some defense related companies are working on what they could have open if they win a contract or not so be sure to ask if they have the contract or if they are bidding on a contract.

Network and Talk all the time! Don't stop, even when you get a great job, continue to build your network and develop your personal brand. Then.....send the elevator back down, right? That is what I am attempting to do with this sage advice to my fellow Patriots.

W – What do you want to do?

This is a VERY difficult question, especially if you are not familiar with the positions and the normal qualifications expected in that position. If you are a Nurse in the military, chances are you will not be one outside of the military if you haven't achieved the education and qualifications needed for civilian nursing positions. Equally, you can't think that an Operations positions in the military is equal to an Operations position in the civilian sector. Do your homework and know at least 2-3 general roles where you know you are a competitive candidate and you have the civilian-equivalent qualifications/experiences to be a competitive candidate.

O– Opportunities

Listen to ALL opportunities -

Sometimes the name of the position sounds "beneath" your level of skill or experience but when you conduct the deep-dive, you may find it is exactly where you need to look at starting your next career as a launch point for that company. Attend hiring events and conferences and yes, you will get the standard "please go to our website". Get their information, card, phone number, email, etc and ask if it is ok if you can follow up with them to ensure your application went through. What I have seen from the many, many career fair and hiring conferences I have attended, very little hiring actually happens at all. Use these events to increase your NETWORKING skills!

Beware! Some of the "on-the-spot offers" I have seen are sometimes for positions that turnover frequently or always need fresh people. Do your homework on the companies attending the event and find out what positions on the websites they always seem to be looking to fill. When you meet new people, ask them what they do and ask questions about how they do it and what keeps them at their current company. A recent survey showed that

68% of new hires of transitioning military members will leave their first post-military job after one year. They took the job to have a job, didn't understand what the job was responsible for, or were sold a bill of goods by one of those companies with high turnover positions----don't be that statistic! Do your homework!

R– References/Recommendations (LinkedIn), Relocation, Resume,

I cannot stress LinkedIn connections, endorsements, and recommendations enough. LinkedIn has become the digital brand of your working image. Prospective companies use LinkedIn as a primary tool (through keyword and Boolean searches) and pay a lot of money to find candidates that have the certain traits that a Hiring Manager is looking for in their next employee. Your LinkedIn profile is a living, breathing document that you need to look at frequently. Another Military Veteran and good friend recommended two books for me to update my LinkedIn profile. It works! (Thanks Joe Frankie)

Relocation is a pretty important topic -

I am asked weekly to help someone find a position in this location or that location since it is where they have to be for this reason or that reason. Later I see messages where they are expressing their frustration on not being able to find a job comparable to their skills, abilities, experience and they have to settle. My word to you is to go where your best opportunity is waiting for you. Personally, I could not find a position in Houston, TX that I felt was my long-term fit but did find that position in Detroit, MI, where I am at now. If you are serious enough about planning the rest of your career, then be ready to move where that perfect job needs you to be at this point in your career. Even a company's current employees know (just like in the military) they will eventually have to move to get to a higher position.

Pay a professional to do your resume –

My recommendation is to pay a professional service to make a resume for you and in the industry terms you need to use for the job/industry you want to join. Try to find a service that specializes in Military to Civilian resume writing but also look to see if they have experience in an industry (automotive, airline, government, oil/gas, etc). There are quite a few Military to Civilian resume writers so be careful and do your homework. I selected a service that also enhanced my LinkedIn profile, several job boards, and also created a Word and PDF resume for Government and another one for an industry. Please just don't pick the first one you see, years of experience doesn't mean they are the best at what they do.

K– Key People, Key Skills, Knowledge

Research your network!

Get to know those who have connected with you. I receive messages daily from people I really don't know at all asking me to vouch for them to some Hiring Manager so they can get an interview or a job. I don't know you so how can I recommend you? I can guess at what you did in your military career from your assignments, awards, schools but my recommendation is something I believe has a value on it so I don't spend it freely. Send that person a message and ask them how they are doing, ask for tips on the company or how they like working at that company; they might be looking to leave too, right? Get a little bit of a relationship and then ask them to help you out with a recommendation.

Highlight what you do, what you are good at, and how you are good at it. There is a section in your profile where you can tell your story or experiences so do it! Use as many words as you can, when recruiters are using key word searches, you want your profile at the top of the list. Please, please, please remember that a recruiter manages multiple openings in addition to conducting phone screenings, multiple candidate phone calls, Hiring Manager briefings, what the company requires of them, and then their own professional development so please don't send a message asking them to "review your profile and let you know where you would best fit in their organization". If a recruiter has that much time available, then their company either isn't hiring much right now or they have given the workload to a recruiter they know will give them good candidates and not this one.

Display your knowledge! I have a friend who is an IT Analyst but their LinkedIn profile looks bland, boring, and has ZERO examples of their competencies. He and I are now working together to improve his digital ID Card. The IT field is HIGHLY competitive so why would a company even interview an IT Analyst who can't make his own digital brand look impeccable? Use LinkedIn to highlight what you know, who you know, and most importantly how you will be an absolute asset to a future employer.

I– Which Industry? Introductions

Study the industries that interest you –

   Use an audible book or actually read a book. I had a chance to be in the Oil and Gas industry so I learned the history of Oil and Gas so I could at least talk the talk in an interview and conditioned my resume to fit some of the positions I was interested in filling. I am now in the Automotive Industry so guess what? Yup, you got it, to date I have finished three novels on the history of the Automobile Industry. Now when I talk to some of the very, very tenured workers in my company I can bring some interesting facts to the conversation. Be passionate about what you do or find something else to do!

Once you decide on the Industry, then decide where in the industry you want to begin. A small company (startup), mid-size (services) company, or a large company (manufacturer or producer) and once you have done that then select the top three you would like to work for and start developing those LinkedIn conversations and contacts so one day, when you are ready, you can ask that contact to help you get an interview! Once you get a little fish on LinkedIn and develop a small relationship, ask if they can introduce you to a bigger fish, and so on. Spend the time investment, I don't see a Fortune 100 CEO pinging you back because you InMailed them about your great qualifications out of nowhere. You will probably receive a different result if you can put a familiar name to the CEO with your story.

N– No Acronyms, No Jargon

I started out as an 11B with the 82nd Airborne Division, spent two years as Platform Instructor for WLC and ALC teaching leadership, was drafted into being a Detailed 79R as a SSG in which I ultimately stayed and converted to Permanent Cadre and retired as a CSM. I specialize in Leadership and want to be a Program Manager. Sound familiar, confused? No kidding...believe it or not, these are the messages my non-veteran coworkers get from transitioning military. Once the message comes in, my coworkers then come to me asking for my deciphering skills. I don't mind converting your coded messages (job security for me, right?) but what if my company didn't have someone like me to advocate for you and to tell coworkers what you actually did in industry terms? You would be immediately upset because you just received ANOTHER "thanks for applying but we went with a more qualified candidate" electronic response. I know, I still have over 3,000 of them in my Yahoo "Employment" folder from the six months I spent looking for a job when I retired from Active Duty.

I want to be a Program Manager…..of what? We all have managed programs but this is a different arena. You need to know how this company makes its bottom line. What are the products, processes, procedures, profits, people? Even after retiring as an E-9, Command Sergeant Major, I had to put my pride and my shadowbox down and start again. I took a job as a low-level employee not even making close to what I made on Active Duty and after a couple of years….I am now a Program Manager in Talent Acquisition, in the Automotive Industry….NOW I get it and yes, the lessons were quite painful.

G– Make time for the Gym

Make time for the Gym…..maintaining your fitness is very important –

Especially in the first year. Your stress will be sky high, different demands, different problems, and also having to adapt to a civilian workforce. Don't worry, I am still impressed with the caliber of the coworkers I have been blessed to work alongside of, and my current bosses, I would put them next to any great leader I ever had in the military. Try your best to maintain the personal lifestyle you had in the military, if you normally rise at 0500 then do that on the weekdays while searching for a job and then in the new job for a bit until you get a routine.

Try to find a way to minimize as many changes to your lifestyle as possible until you get the hang of this new environment. Yes, there are bosses on the outside who think you need to be accessible 24/7 and even if this is the case, the stress is nowhere it was in the military. If you get good at what you do, then you will get a vote faster than you think. Several transitioning military members I have brought into my current organization are already promoted to being a manager and all of them are doing extremely well in their new careers.

Just throwing this part in here...companies have varying dress codes...I only have one. Dress every day for where you want to be, not where you are. If you have to wear a uniform, then wear it better than anyone else.

Now that I have walked you through the N-E-T-W-O-R-K-I-N-G aspect of this book, there are some addition points that I have learned along the way.

Company Transition/Reception –

Coming into a company for the first time can be a traumatic event for the transitioning Veteran and will immediately set the stage on whether the Veteran will choose to stay with the company long-term or immediately begin looking for employment elsewhere. Veterans have been trained for many years in the six P's of planning (Prior Planning Prevents Piss Poor Performance). We have been trained for years to immediately begin developing a plan and a backup plan when we notice things may not be advantageous to our current situation. It has been said (unverified by me) that up to 68% of transitioning Service Members will leave their first job out of the military within the first 12 months of employment. Companies should ask themselves "Why?" if this is happening to them. What I have personally seen in the period since my transition is:

Overselling the job –

Companies can do better at who they send from their Talent Acquisition departments. In some cases, companies will hire a few folks from a local temp agency to dawn a company t-shirt, stand in for them and take resumes. It is the job of a recruiter/recruiting manager to know their company and to be able to accurately explain a "day in the life" of their positions. Too many times I have heard from Veterans the job isn't what was told to them, the bonus structure, the pay, the benefits were not what they were supposed to be when they accepted the position. The companies presenting themselves to hire Veterans should understand that most of the transitioning Service Members have never held a professional level civilian position and even the slightest things can be overlooked. Things like expected pay dates, health/dental care, job or position requirements, workhours, bonus structures, etc. Veterans take a job because they have a tendency to believe what is being told to them and when they find out it was even partially untrue, they will immediately begin to separate themselves from that environment. Be careful of organizations who immediately promote how "fun" their work environments will be. You will see them, they bring a lot of "fun" people to every single conference. I come to mentor and if we have matching interests as a candidate and as a potential employer then we can discuss the seriousness of our work.

Veteran undervalue –

Transitioning Service Members really need to sit-down with a mentor and conduct a true assessment of what they are worth in today's workforce. Too many times I have seen Veterans over/undervalue themselves and either miss out on great opportunities or let themselves, unwittingly, be taken advantage of by some companies unintentionally.

Tax break advantages and Quotas –

Under today's current tax structure, companies hiring recently separated Veterans (three years and less) can experience a significant tax incentive for placing newly separated Veterans in their ranks. Whenever I see a slogan like "we will hire 25,000 Veterans" I tend to become very cautious. They probably have the right intentions but it does cause me to ask myself two questions. Are they doing this as a form of revenue for the company in tax incentives and, most importantly, what did they do with the last 25,000 Veterans they hired? Do they have that much turnover?

Lack of Mentorship –

In the Army, the Senior Non-Commissioned Officers are responsible for the Army Sponsorship Program. This program is designed to help transition in a new arrival to the unit. We would establish contact prior to the new Soldier leaving their old unit, maintain contact throughout the transition period, and then receive them when they arrived at the new duty station. Once they were at their new until, they were immediately assigned a mentor for the first period of the new assignment/new role until they established their own connections and got their "legs up under them". It didn't always happen that way but when it did, it worked like a thing of beauty. This is what I recommend companies do in receiving Veterans, even older Veterans who believe they don't need sponsorship. Does it work? As of today, my organization has retained over 95% of the new hires that I have personally brought in to my organization.

Dress –

Short subject from what I have learned through trial and error. My current company has one dress code.....Dress Appropriately. Although it is simple, it can be challenging to a newly transitioned Veteran since we really don't know what is appropriate for all settings in a new work environment. To help ease this for me, I tend to dress one level above what I believe is appropriate for the situation. If it is a business casual situation where polo shirts and slacks would work, I will wear a starched long sleeve shirt with pressed slacks. If it is a company outing with t-shirts and blue jeans, then I will wear pressed blue jeans and a polo shirt, you can get the drift of what I am saying. In the Veteran's closest should be at least two pair of tan, blue, black, and grey slacks.

There should also be two different styles of various colors of shirts in long sleeve and polo. Most important to me, is three suits consisting of blue, black, and gray. Once you have these items, there isn't a situation you would not be prepared to attend. Just like our uniforms, always ensure your suits are tailored to fit (with room for expansion), pressed, and ready to go at a moment's notice. You don't have to spend a lot of money on dry cleaning, even today, I really only take my suits to the cleaners. The rest of my work clothes, I pull out the ironing board and starch and get them done while I am watching a movie or sports on the weekend. Companies have varying dress codes...I only have one. Dress every day for where you want to be, not where you are. If you have to wear a uniform, then wear it better than anyone else.

Interviewing – RELAX!!!

I know this is tougher than you think. I work with recruiters and hiring managers everyday. They don't like interviewing anymore than you like being interviewed. Try to have a decent time in the interview and if they don't want to have one then that could be a sign this fit may not be for you. The biggest complaint that I get from hiring mangers is that Veterans do not openly talk about themselves and they are right. We are taught to talk about our units, our teams, our brothers and sisters-in-arms. It is very taboo in the military to simply talk about your individual accomplishments since it can be seen as boasting or bragging. I work with those managers to (since they need to know what you are capable of) to get the Veteran to talk about their teams, their unit's accomplishments and the say something like "and what was your role in that?". The biggest comments I hear from hiring managers are:

They really didn't show me they know how to do the job

They were really stiff and militaristic

They had really short answers

They seemed like they just wanted the interview to be over

They don't seem like they would be happy in that job

You have to practice your answers. Most companies use a format called S-T-A-R which is Situation, Task, Action, and Result. This is where you will get the dreaded "Tell me about a time....". They are simply looking to see if you are capable of handling a situation that is important to them. A question I hear a lot is "Tell me about a time you worked with someone you didn't get along with and still had a job to do". We have all experienced this one but Veterans will immediately say something like I try to get along with everyone which is not the right answer. They are looking for you to say something along the lines of "That person and I were able to resolve our differences and put our work ahead of any other grievances for the good of the project". They just want to know if you will get the job done.

The Offer / Competing Offers –

The Offer of Employment can be a very confusing time for the transitioning Service Member and even a Veteran who has already transitioned and is now finding another position. What I advise is for the offer letter, you have to look beyond the stated salary. What other benefits come with the employment with this organization? How much of the health/dental/vision premiums are covered by the company and how much will my average co-pays be for medical visits? It doesn't do much good to have a great annual salary if you have higher benefit costs that you will have to pay out of pocket. You will find that most Contractor organizations do provide benefits and a great salary but the trade off is that their benefits are higher for your out of pocket.

Established, large companies have better bargaining power with insurance companies and are able to get lower costs because of the sizes of their plans. Smaller companies do not have this bargaining power which means higher costs that may be passed on to you. In a larger company if your offered starting salary is $85k and the general out of pocket cost for benefits is relatively low, then you will get to keep most of your annual salary. If the other offer letter is $100k, sure it looks better but in reality, your will only realize an annual salary of $75k due to the higher cost of your benefits and now a higher tax bracket.

Do your research and don't go by just what the annual salary will be. Most of the larger companies have 401k, health, dental, vision, tuition reimbursement, life insurance, and short/long-term disability. What is your per-paycheck cost to participate in these plans. Your recruiter should be able to provide this information to you. Questions you should ask:

When do the benefits start?

Am I covered before I am able to select which plans I want participate in?

What percentage is the employer contribution to the benefit premiums? (this is important to know in case you lose your job and are offered the chance to continue your benefits until you get another coverage plan – Look up COBRA)

What is the employer contribution for the 401k?

When am I considered "vested" for the money in my 401K?

What are the stipulations on tuition reimbursement? Can I pick my degree plan or does it have to be in line with my job to be covered?

What are the requirements for payout of short and long term disability?

Recruiters and Resumes –

"I have applied to 10 jobs with this company and have never received an answer", sound familiar? Why is it that recruiters don't contact us? Why do our applications go into a black hole never to be heard from again? Let me break it down for you.

Number one thing I want to get out there is that recruiters work their tails off. The professionals I have had the privilege of working with and next to since I retired from the Army are second to none. They are a requisition carrying, interview coordinating, phone call making, meeting coordinating, family balancing machine and they have my upmost respect! People in Talent Acquisition have been among the hardest working folks I have ever seen and the leaders are second to none (Kim H., Pat S., Mark M., Steve F., Rick K. – and only one of them is a Veteran).

A recruiter is a Human Resources representative and depending on how long that recruiter has worked in that industry and for that company has A LOT to do with what they do with your application. No doubt that some of us are very qualified to do the jobs we have applied to fill but is our resume "readable" to a recruiter who is not an expert in the position you are trying to fill? Here's how it goes.....A hiring manager has a new position or an employee has recently left. The hiring manager contacts the recruiter and says "hey, I have a position to fill". The recruiter and the hiring manager exchange the position necessities and the requirements the candidates need to have for the hiring manage to consider an interview with them. These are called Minimum Requirements and Preferred/Recommended Requirements.

The process here is simple, if you don't meet all the Minimum Requirements, don't apply for the position. By law, each person interviewed for this position must meet all Minimum Requirements or the company could be subject to legal action for whatever discriminatory claims may come their way if they hired someone unqualified over someone that was qualified according to the job posting.

Now, what is the recruiter looking for? First you have to realize, the bigger the company the bigger the workload for a recruiter. Workloads are called a requisition load since a job fill request is called a requisition, most recruiters have a requisition load of 40-70 requisitions and each requisition usually has anywhere from 1-5 positions. So, let's do the math. Say an average requisition has 3 vacancies that must be filled then the recruiter is attempting to fill 120 – 210 positions within the next 30-45 days.

Each requisition can get around 300 candidates depending on the company so that is 12,000 applications on the low end and 21,000 applications on the high end. Even if the recruiter is using a Keyword search, it is a very daunting task to find a candidate slate of 3-5 candidates per position that the hiring manager would be happy with to interview and possible find their dream candidate. I am sure a lot of you will argue with my numbers since we are all in very different environments but hey, I had to make a point somewhere for the understanding.

So now, being reasonable, what are the odds that recruiter will actually get to your application? What are the odds they will reach out to you for a phone call? What are your odds that you will receive that wanted discussion with that recruiter on how or why you were not selected and how you can improve your resume for a better chance next time? Of course, it is slim to none. Even if the recruiter has years in that industry, knows his/her positions inside and out, you have a low chance of being selected especially if the recruiter cannot understand your jargon filled, militaristic resume.

This is why the "Friend of a friend" stuff is alive and well in Corporate America even today. We have all of these systems and processes in place to ensure we are doing our best for the fair and equitable treatment of all candidates but at the end of the day, the hiring manager needs candidates like yesterday and the recruiter wants to make that happen for them since their hiring managers' opinion has a lot to do with the recruiter's job rating. Having been part of Talent Acquisition for over 25 years now I can say sure, we can do better but each improvement in the area costs the company a lot of money. HR is a cost to the company and does not generate a profit so in lean times, systems and processes that cost more money are typically put on the back burner.

This is why Networking is at the crux of a successful transition and a successful career, you need to develop your brand, you need others to say "I know a person" when that vacancy comes up. Not that you are guaranteed to be selected for the role after you interviewed but at least you will probably be interviewed! Then when you do get that elusive interview.....don't blow it by not being prepared like I have in the past.

Act like the Natives / Play the Game –

I met with a Veteran who contacted me on LinkedIn. It was my first time meeting him in person even though we had exchanged a few messages here and there over a six month period. This time, the Veteran contacted me and said he really needed someone to talk to and of course, that launched me into action of when and where? So, we met up and he begins telling me how he doesn't like his company, his job, and how he is capable of so much more. He feels as though he is being constrained and his talents are not being used....they just don't "get" him.

After he spoke for a while, what I realized is simply that they weren't the ones who needed an adjustment, he was. I asked him why he left the military, why he moved to his current location, why he took his current position. Most importantly, I asked him why he was trying to make his company fit into his view instead of him fitting into theirs. We left the military for whatever reason, so why are we trying to make everyone fit into a military view of life and our work environment? In leaving the military we made a decision to "divorce" the military (or they made the decision for us); we are now civilians. Why aren't we trying harder to understand how they work instead of why they aren't like us?

We, as Veterans, need to do a better job of involving ourselves into our current environment instead of complaining why our situation isn't the way we want it to be. So, I asked him, if less than 5% of the nation's population has served in the military, why are you acting like the other 95% have? It is only normal that in some situations we may not appear to fit in because WE ARE different, we have been exposed to different environments, different opportunities, different regimes than the other 95% of the population. Do your homework and see if the problem is with you before you claim everyone else is "messed up".

Send the elevator back down –

Companies are getting on board with having someone, a Military Advocate, or a section in place to focus on Veteran hiring initiatives. In this, a person (usually a Veteran but not always) is tasked with focusing on the Military Veteran population and ensuring the organization finds better ways to create opportunities for transitioning Service Members. I will say (some will be offended) not all Military Advocates perform at the same level. I can say this with a matter of authenticity from the countless Veterans and Service Members who have contacted me and expressed their frustration of attempting to reach out by message and phone to these Military Advocates only to never receive so much as a response.

I spent almost 25 years of my life in uniform and did my best to take care of my soldiers and their families. I can't say I was the best at it but I can say that I cared about my Soldiers, their families, and my Army. Sometimes the Soldier won, sometimes the family won, and sometimes the Army won in certain situations but at the end of the day, I made decisions based on what I believe was in the best interest of all three. This continues for me today but now there are other dynamics, best interest of the Service Member (all branches), their family situation, my employer, and the Veteran Community.

Yes, there are days I could have done more in my current and previous Advocate roles, but in most of my days I am satisfied that I am doing all that I can do on a personal and professional level to advance the causes of our transitioning Service Members, their families, and the Veteran Community. I can't say that is the norm in today's transition environment, there are some very fortunate folks sitting in these Military Advocate positions, that although their intentions may be honorable, are not the right folks for that position.

Companies must ensure two primary things when selecting a person to fill this role. One, that person must have the knowledge, skills, and experiences to be able to represent the Military Community as a whole to the employer. They must be aware of current trends, issues, and obstacles placed in front of those transitioning Warriors that may inhibit their readiness to complete a successful transition from the military to a civilian work environment. That person must have a good working knowledge of all the branches, all the jobs, all the schools, all the assignments, and all of the promotion systems the military has to be able to gauge what would be a great fit into their current organization from a professional and cultural fit; this person's professional opinions must warrant respect across the Military Community and the Corporate Communities.

The second part of the this is that person selected to be a Military Advocate must also have the business knowledge and awareness to be able to speak with a matter of authority on what is a good fit for the long-term needs of the company. Understanding the industry, the organization, and the business climate will help open doors with hiring managers who will need to be convinced to "take a chance" on a Military Candidate who may have the educational requirements of the industry but does not have the industry experience they are looking for and that they will be worth the investment of time and training that will have to be allocated to them. We simply cannot continue to place just anyone in these very important positions since they are viewed as the representative of the military community and of the company to the transitioning Service Members.

So, if you are one of the lucky ones who have been placed in this key position, please realize how fortunate you are to be in that position and that, most importantly, you are setting the stage for thousands of transitioning Service Members in how they will be viewed, accepted, promoted, or fired over the next 10-20 years. Please never take this position lightly, pick up your phone and return a call, return a message. We are all counting on you to take care of our Warriors and their families. The person selected for this position, unfortunately, must also be aware of candidates who do not represent themselves accurately, who may have served but did not do the things they are saying they did, or even worse, they did not actually serve at all.

Over the last few years I have encountered candidates who claimed to be military veterans who never served at all, Veterans who claimed to have been awarded the Medal of Honor but was not, claimed to have been Commissioned Officers but were not, and claimed to have led hundreds of troops but did not. The person who serves as a Military Advocate has an obligation to protect the integrity of the Veteran Community and to protect the company they work for from hiring an unqualified person into a role they never should have had in the first place which will ultimately tarnish the reputation of all Veterans and will cost the company money down the road when the truth comes out.

Hiring Conferences –

If you believe you will find a great job and have it offered to you at a hiring conference then you will probably be very disappointed. As a rule, hiring managers usually do not attend hiring conference and/or job fairs. Companies will typically staff these tables with recruiters, interns, temps, and maybe a Veteran or two who now work at the company. Over the last few hiring conferences I have attended on behalf of my employer, they have given me the ability to bring two hiring managers and two recruiters with me to be able to conduct actual job interviews and to extend real offers of employment on the spot. This is NOT typical of companies.

Beware of the companies that are ready to extend an offer to you at the conference. These offers are usually for very high-turnover positions they know they will have a vacancy for in the future because people do not stay in those position for whatever reason. Beware of "job interviews" that are not being conducted by actual hiring managers. If you are extended an invitation to interview at a conference, ask for the person's information before agreeing to the interview. Who are they in the company, do they work in recruiting, human resources, or are they actually in the business unit with a real hiring need? Does the position you are interviewing for have a complete job description and can I find it currently being advertised online?

Most companies will conduct one and up to four very lengthy interviews with candidates before selecting a candidate for hire along with some type of cultural or personality assessment for fit. Hiring a new employee is a costly endeavor for an organization and those who are doing it right take some time to do this. Don't take the first thing that comes your way without doing research in the position, the team, the company, the industry, and the location. Companies come to these events because they want to be known as supporting Veterans but not all companies and/or positions are created equal. If someone is offering you a lot of money and an on-the-spot offer with a limited interview, those are very big red flags. There's a reason why it is said that up to 68% of new Veteran hires leave their first position in the first 12 months, try not to be one of those statistics and do your homework up front.

For-Profit Placements and Contractor companies –

For-profit companies make money by finding you a position in a company. Their business model is to be paid up to a certain percentage of your first year's annual salary once you are placed. Business is business and if you use these organizations to find a great job, in a great industry, in a great location then more power to you and then but also understand they have agreements with companies to do this type of business with them and in some cases, will steer you into those companies.

I am contacted, almost daily, with for-profit companies who want to showcase a Veteran to us in hopes that we will interview and place the Veteran. These are honorable people doing honorable work so please do not think otherwise, it is simply a business model.

The other side of the "for-profit" is a contractor company. These companies usually have an agreement with larger organizations to provide temporary labor when the need arises. Let's look at the Automotive Industry.....for example, a business model is that a certain company will need 100 people to staff a project. The company has 60 fulltime employees they can dedicate to the project but will need 40 similarly qualified workers to fully staff the project but will no longer need them once the project has ended. In this case, the larger company will submit a requisition need to the contractor companies for 40 contract workers. The contract workers will typically work onsite alongside of the fulltime workers, will have badge access, laptops, and phones (just as the fulltime workers) but once the project is over they are either moved to another project or let go.

For transitioning Service Members, this is a golden opportunity to get your foot in the door with the larger companies. Contract companies can provide benefits to you (usually at a higher cost than being a direct employee of the larger company) and can give you valuable industry experience. In a lot of cases, while working as a contractor, when the larger company has an opening for a new fulltime employee, the hiring manager will typically look at their contract force to see who is available for hire before they will look outside of the organization.

If you are offered a position with a contract company, don't be so quick to turn those down and listen to what opportunities they have with various industries as you may be able to get experience with several industries all while having stability with the contract company. These companies will typically have a hiring clause in the master agreement with the larger company that they cannot hire a contractor to a direct hire position unless some condition has been met which is usually a time factor or a placement fee the company will need to collect before letting you go.

VEVRA of 2013 –

Before I begin this conversation, I will direct you to look up The Vietnam Era Veterans Readjustment Act of 2013 (VEVRA) on your own and become familiar with it. This section is only to give you a very high-level view of this piece of legislation and is not intended to portray me as an expert on this Act. I do believe it is something that should be briefed to all Service Members, long before they begin their transition out of the military. This Act, is a revision of the 1973 act that was put in place by Congress at the end of the

Vietnam War once it was identified that our Vietnam Veterans were paying a heavy price for the unpopular conflict in high unemployment rates and pay disparity.

Congress recognized that companies were not hiring our Vietnam Veterans at a similar rate of Non-Veterans and when they were offered a position, there were a lot of times where the pay was significantly lower than other newly hired employees. In my opinion, during that time, we were also standing up the new All Volunteer Armed Forces and we very well couldn't expect a lot of volunteers if they had poor employment prospects once they left the military.

So, Congress enacted the Vietnam Era Veterans Readjustment Act which gave specific rules and guidance to those companies performing under contracts with the U.S. Government to establish benchmarks and hiring initiatives to employ our Veterans once they left the military. Years later, the same disparity occurred referencing our Post 9-11 Veterans. In one example, the U.S. general unemployment rate was 3-4% below that of the Post 9-11 Veteran unemployment rate so the Act was revised to include our Post 9-11 Veterans into this protected status.

The VEVRA establishes recommended actions to be taken by companies performing under government contracts in the outreach, hiring, selection, promotion, retention, and termination of Protected Military Veterans. The Act sets four Protected Veteran Categories and gives companies the option to use a general benchmark (provided by the Government) or to research their own labor markets to create their own benchmark in hiring Protected Veterans. At this writing, the current general benchmark is 6.4%. This means that companies doing business with the U.S. Government should goal their hiring efforts for Protected Veterans at 6.4% of their total hires. This is also advised to be broken down and applied by location if the company has multiple locations around the U.S.

So, what are the Protected Veteran categories? First is a Disabled Veteran, the rule here is a Veteran who has been Medically Discharged from the military for injuries occurring during Military Service, or has a 30% or higher disability rating from the Veterans Affairs, or has a 20% or higher rating with a significantly life-altering disability such as loss of a limb. Second category is the Recently Separated Veteran which covers Military Veterans discharged for anything other than a Dishonorable Discharge for their first three years after separation from the military.

The third protected category is a Wartime/Campaign Medal Veteran which most of us commonly refer to as a Combat Veteran. These Veterans were awarded a medal signifying their service during a period of armed conflict. The last and fourth protected category is the Service Medal Veteran which was enacted in 1996 under President Clinton to recognize the service of our military that served during a period of conflict and worked directly in support of that conflict but may not have deployed in direct action of the conflict.

All of these Protected Veteran categories and the benchmarks are the primary reason why companies are now creating positions for and hiring Military Advocates. Among some of the items specifically prohibited by the Act is the discussion of any benefits a person receives as a result of their military service. This includes any talk of retirement money, disability compensation, GI Bill income, etc. This is in place because some companies were hiring Veterans at a salary lower than their civilian counterparts because they had other money coming in so the company benefited by gaining a similarly qualified person at a lower salary.

Senior NCO's and Officers –

Our categories are the absolute toughest to find a position of employment. In essence, you will be hard pressed to find a position that is anywhere near similar in responsibility and authority as what you have or had in the military. Civilians have a hard time grasping the pure scope, size, and complexity of our positions. When I speak with Senior NCO's and Senior Officers and I ask them what they want to do the usual reply is they want to be a Director or a Program Manager. Then I say "of what? "and that is where the stump comes in.

Unless you are taking a government position or a defense role of some type, you probably will not be a Director or even a Program Manager. This is the equivalent of a civilian who had worked 20 years in an industry and now wants to join the military saying to you "I want to be the XO or the Operations Sergeant Major". What are they missing? You know as well as I do, they are missing the years of experience in the industry. They would also be jumping over how many Service Members who have worked their whole careers for that promotion? And then, even if we did give that position to them, would they be able to effectively handle the day to day business of the military without the experience and understanding that a XO or an Operations Sergeant Major has? Of course they wouldn't do very well at all.

I advise my Senior NCO's and Senior Officers that I work with to consider starting off as an Individual Contributor role to learn the business, the industry, the geo-political realm of this new environment and when the time is right, then submit your name for the Director or Program Manager role. Be wary of companies that want to bring you straight in to those roles since you have to remember, the people who will be working for you wanted that role too so there will probably be some friction when you get there.

Conclusion –

Eventually I met a lady (who is now my wife) who didn't care about money, she was a joy to be around and liked watching TV or a movie (since it was all I could really afford). One day she said she wanted to stop by a restaurant for a friend's birthday and asked if it would be ok and I assured here it was (not really but hey, it's dating, right?) Then it happened, finally, I struck up a conversation with someone else who seemed like they were bored and through a series of events...she became my boss which eventually led to my position today and my eventual move out of Houston to Detroit.

When I tell you that I understand your employment struggle, I do truly understand more than you can realize. The frustration, the calls, the applications, the "hey, we'll be in contact", and then the voicemail answers, over and over again. I truly hope that in writing this advice to you, that in some small way, I can make a difference in the way our transitioning military members and their families are treated by our own Service Branches after giving so much during their service to our Nation. I have always said the military will give you 1,000 reasons to stay in but are not very good at helping you get out. I was fortunate, I had a year, although still busy with my duties, and still had a horrible experience.

What about that family that has only a 30, 60, or 90-day notice that their careers are ending? There has to be a change, there has to be a difference made somewhere in the truly depressing cycle that I see over and over again in my position as a Veteran's Hiring Initiatives Program Manager. We must learn to value our soon to be former Military Members just as we do our current Military Members.

Did you know in the military, Officers get a choice during their careers to take time off from the Military Service and go to school for a Master's Degree? Some of these schools are in foreign countries and really cost the U.S. Government a lot of money to house and pay for their education. The Armed Forces should look at doing something equivalent for the Senior Enlisted Corp or letting them participate in a yearlong "Training with Industry" type program.

We don't do enough for our Enlisted Corp and when we are done with them, hopefully they get a plaque, a mug, or some other small treasure and we send them out the door without much preparation at all. Then we wonder just why we have disgruntled former Service Members who really don't want their kids to serve. There must be a fair and equitable trade in that the Service Member held up their end of the bargain, they completed their time and are being Honorably discharged.

We must take better care of them on the way out of the door and quit acting as though a Transition Assistance Program taught at the base by former or present Military Members, who never left the base, are going to give them a great start. Can we look at inserting a Sponsorship program in our local Reserve and National Guard units to welcome those transitioning members and their families into the local area and linking them in with established contacts for employment? Wouldn't this also help the transitioning member also make the decision to become a member of the Guard or Reserve?

When the statement arises, as it will, "We can't afford to keep a Senior NCO or Senior Officer on the books that long" then we need to look at positions where they can still be accountable for earning their paycheck while at the same time allowing them to prepare for a significant shift in their lives. There are plenty of Reserve and National Guard units that would greatly benefit from the advice and training of a Senior leader who could be attached to that unit pending retirement or discharge.

So, if you have read this to the end, then I do appreciate your dedication or boredom (whichever allowed you to have this much time available) ....these thoughts are what I try to express to my fellow brothers and sisters choosing or having to leave their military careers. Every day I train, influence, coach, and mentor hiring managers and recruiters to give our transitioning Military Service Members a shot at an interview. I simply ask that when you do get that elusive interview, don't blow it like I did. Do your homework, pay attention, make those connections and when you have finally arrived at your version of a dream job…..answer your LinkedIn Inbox messages and help that completely stressed out transitioning Warrior get to their dream job. In my opinion, that's the true definition of Veteran's Preference.

I am available if you have no one else to call or you believe you are at the end of hope. You are not alone in this world as long as you have brothers and sisters-in-arms. We do not leave anyone behind.

Benny R. Kinsey, MBA, PMP, PHR, SSBB

Command Sergeant Major (Retired)

(936) 648-7086

Benny.kinsey@yahoo.com

96134933R00026

Made in the USA
Lexington, KY
17 August 2018